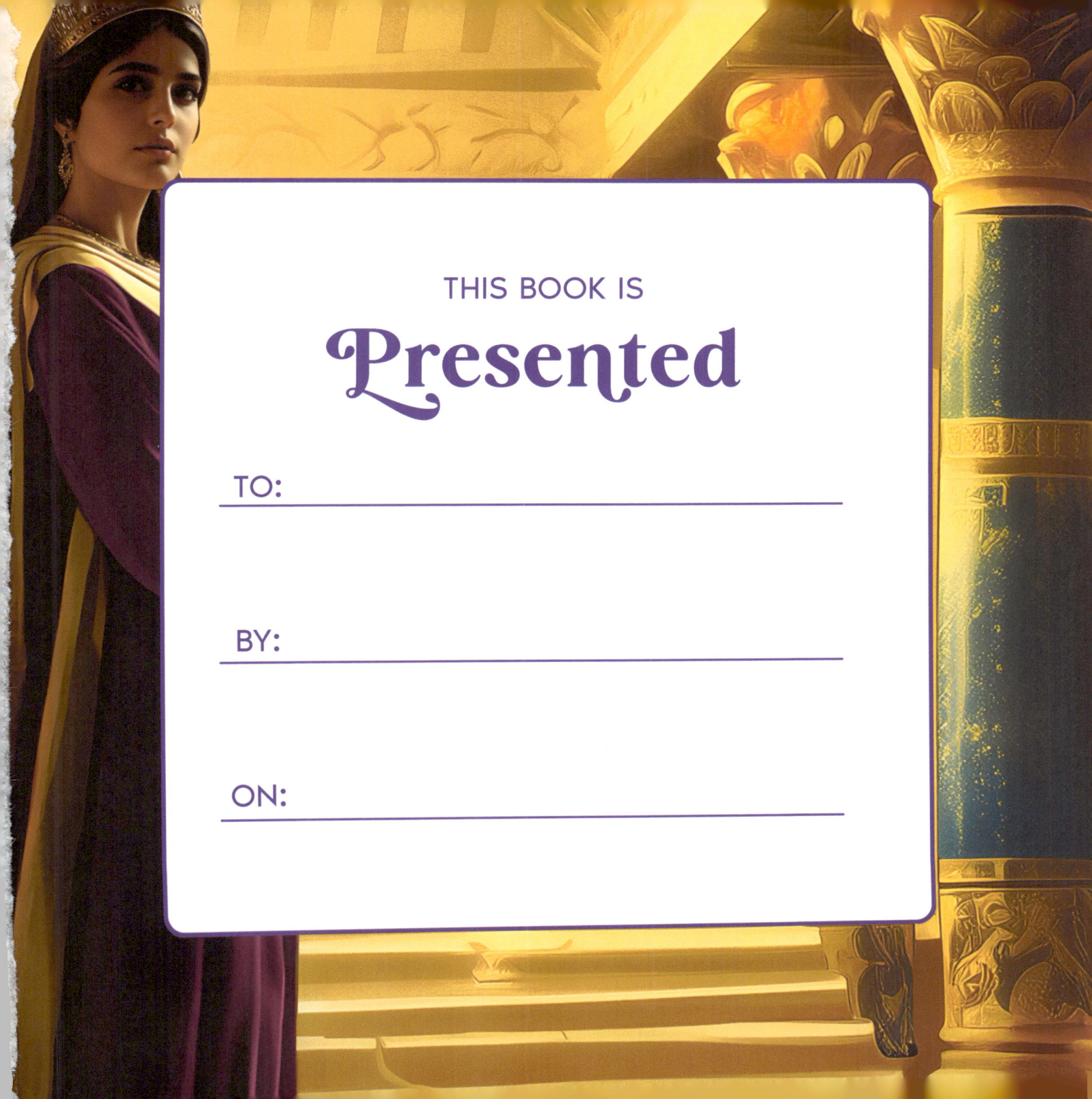

THIS BOOK IS

Presented

TO:
_____

BY:
_____

ON:
_____

Copyright © Arabella Penrose, 2024.

Arabella Penrose: Author, Art Director, Book Design
Frank S. Scavo: Poet, Story Editor, Collaborator
Moazam Bravi: Artwork Editor

All rights reserved. No part of this publication may be reproduced, distributed, or transmitted in any form or by any means, or stored in any database or retrieval system, without prior written permission of the copyright holder.

All inquiries should be directed to:
www.arabellapenrose.com

ISBN-13: 978-1-962924-07-8 - Paperback
ISBN-13: 978-1-962924-08-5 - Hardcover

Scripture quotations marked NLT are taken from the *Holy Bible*, New Living Translation, copyright © 1996, 2004, 2015 by Tyndale House Foundation. Used by permission of Tyndale House Publishers, Inc., Carol Stream, Illinois 60188. All rights reserved.

QUEEN
Esther

A RHYMING BIBLE STORY OF BRAVERY, DETERMINATION, AND RESILIENCE

BY ARABELLA PENROSE

"Who knows if perhaps you were made queen for just such a time as this?"

Esther 4:14b (NLT)

For the boys and girls being raised up in this generation. May God strengthen you to be bold and courageous, just like Esther. He made you "for such a time as this."

In faraway Persia, a kingdom so vast,
Lived Esther, a Jew, many centuries past.
She'd lost both her parents, she was dwelling alone,
So, Mordecai, her cousin, raised her up as his own.

He cared for young Esther like she was his daughter.
They were God's chosen people, as ever he taught her.
"Dear Esther," he said, "We're so far from God's land."
So let us now trust Him, we know not what He's planned."

Read: Esther 2:5-7

Then one day, King Xerxes was seeking a queen. "Bring me the most lovely that you've ever seen."

Mordecai said to Esther, "I know you must go. But that you are a Jew, don't let anyone know."

Read: Esther 2:1-10

She came to the palace, its splendor replete,

For a year they prepared her, King Xerxes to meet.

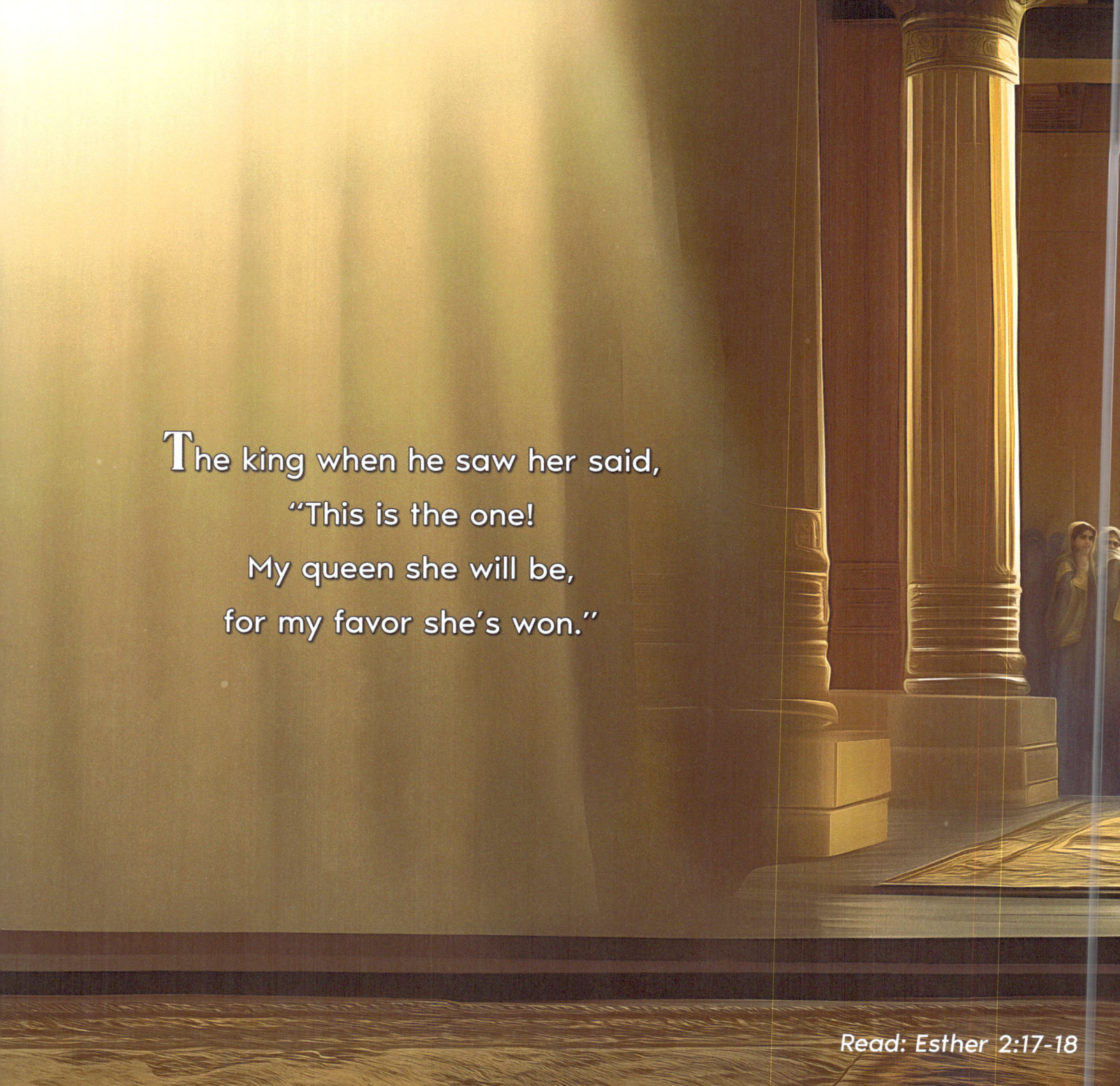

The king when he saw her said,
"This is the one!
My queen she will be,
for my favor she's won."

Read: Esther 2:17-18

Then Mordecai heard of a most evil thing:
Two guards now were planning to murder the king.
He said, "Esther, go tell the king of this plot."
And the king was so grateful the killers were caught.

Read: Esther 2:21-23

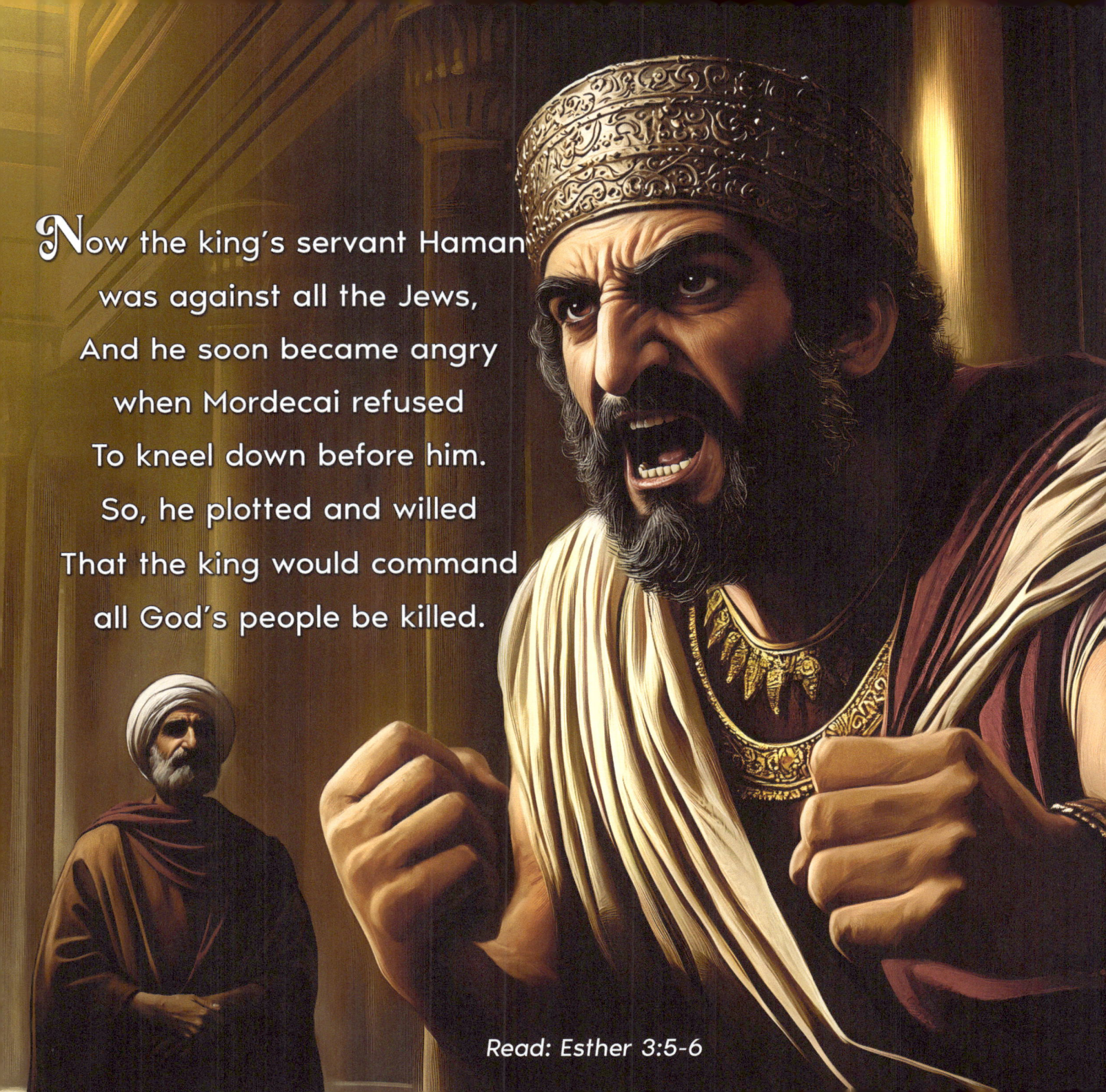

Now the king's servant Haman
was against all the Jews,
And he soon became angry
when Mordecai refused
To kneel down before him.
So, he plotted and willed
That the king would command
all God's people be killed.

Read: Esther 3:5-6

Mordecai sent to Esther the decree the king signed,
And he said, "Beg the king now that he change his mind."
But she could not approach him, she could not draw nigh,
Without his permission, she surely would die.

Read: Esther 4:6-8, 10-11

Mordecai said to Esther, "May we the Lord please.
Perhaps God prepared you for times such as these!"
Queen Esther replied, "Let us fast for three days:
Now gather the Jews and command them to pray."

Read: Esther 4:12-16

And Esther said, "Cousin, I'll do as you say: I will see King Xerxes upon the third day. The Jews are my people, I will not deny. I will not be silent; I'm willing to die."

After three days of prayer, Esther went to the king.
He asked her, "What is this request that you bring?"
She said, "Let's make merry, let's eat and drink wine,
And then I will tell you just what's on my mind."

Read: Esther 5:1-7

The king, full of anger, shouted,
"Who is this man?"
And Esther cried out,
"It's this wicked Haman!"
The king ordered Haman
to then meet his fate,
And that Esther and Mordecai
should take his estate.

Read: Esther 7:5-10, 8:1-2

Mordecai then asked Xerxes for another decree,
That throughout the land all the Jews would be free.
God's people were glad, they were so overjoyed,
That the Lord did protect them, they'd not be destroyed.

Read: Esther 8:3-8, 11-13; 8:20-22

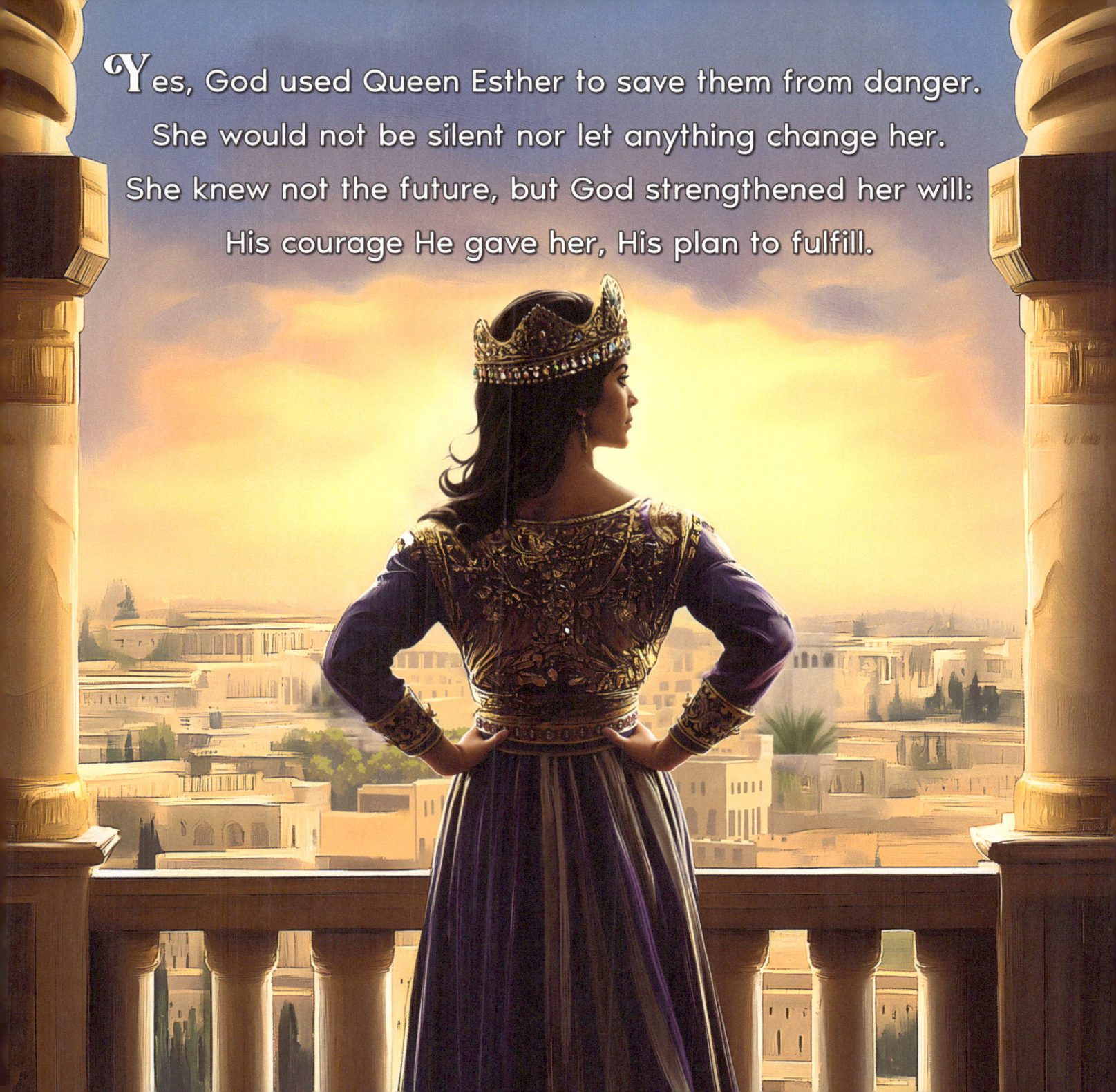

Yes, God used Queen Esther to save them from danger.
She would not be silent nor let anything change her.
She knew not the future, but God strengthened her will:
His courage He gave her, His plan to fulfill.

So, when you're afraid, pray "God give me Your strength,
Let me know Your love in its depth, breadth, and length."
With God's people pray, "Lord, be with us this hour;
Let us know Your purpose, Your plan, and Your power."

So, when you're in danger or trouble appears,
You can, like Queen Esther, tell God all your fears.
God will make a pathway for you to get through:
Just trust in His grace and His great love for you.

Read: Ephesians 3:17-19

Discussion Guide

BRAVERY AND COURAGE

Question: How did Esther show bravery in the story?

Discuss: Esther showed great bravery when she went to the king to save her people, even though it was dangerous. Explain bravery as doing what's right, even when it's scary. Ask your child if they've ever done something brave, like standing up for a friend or trying something new.

TRUSTING GOD'S PLAN

Question: How did Esther trust in God's plan for her?

Discuss: Esther trusted that God had a purpose for her, even when she didn't know what would happen. Talk about how trusting God means believing that He has a good plan for us. Ask your child who they trust and how trusting God can help them feel safe, just like Esther did.

HELPING OTHERS

Question: Why did Esther decide to help God's people?

Discuss: Esther loved her people and wanted to protect them, even if it was dangerous for her. Talk about why it's important to help others, even when it's hard. Encourage your child to think of ways they can help others, like sharing or being kind to someone who's feeling left out.

DETERMINATION

Question: How did Esther show determination?

Discuss: Esther didn't give up, even when the task was difficult. Discuss determination as trying your best and sticking with something. Ask your child about times when they didn't give up, like learning a new skill or finishing a tough project.

RESILIENCE

Question: How did Esther stay strong and not give up?

Discuss: Esther faced many challenges but stayed strong and courageous. Explain resilience as the ability to keep going even when things are tough. Encourage your child to share a time they showed resilience, such as solving a problem or practicing something until they got better, even if, at first, they failed.

GOD'S PURPOSE

Question: What special purpose did God have for Esther?

Discuss: God placed Esther as queen to save His people. Discuss the idea that God has a special purpose for everyone., whether it be great or small Ask your child what they think their special purpose could be and remind them that, like Esther, they can trust God to guide them.

ROLE MODEL

Question: If you could be like Esther in one way, what would it be?

Discuss: Discuss things like bravery, determination, and resilience. Encourage your child to choose something about Esther's character and talk about how they might use it in their own life, whether at school, home, or with friends.

TO GET **FREE PRINTABLE DOWNLOADS**
OF THE DISCUSSION GUIDE AND OTHER FREE RESOURCES,
GO TO MY **WEBSITE:** **WWW.ARABELLAPENROSE.COM**

About the Series

In a world filled with conflicting messages about femininity, the Real Women Heroes of the Bible series brings biblical role models to life for today's generation. Told in rhyming verse, each book tells of a different biblical heroine, showcasing their unique virtues and traits. The series features realistic illustrations that convey these are real women, not fairy tales. By exploring the lives of these women God intentionally chose to be featured in His Word, young girls can find godly examples of womanhood and be inspired to develop their own God-given strengths. Most importantly, they will understand that the very best models for what it means to be a woman can be found in the pages of the Bible. Each heroine's faith-filled life carries powerful lessons that will speak to the hearts of girls today.

About the Author

Since childhood, Arabella has always loved poetry and dreamed of one day publishing her own poems. She splits her time between her native Southern California and Southern Spain. After earning her Bachelor of Arts from UC Santa Barbara, Arabella worked as a translator and a teacher. But her true passion is to nurture the hearts of children through stories. In her spare time, you can find Arabella hiking or walking the beach with her pup, Snoopy, and spending time with her son, Mateo. Arabella draws inspiration from her father, who instilled in her a love of poetry and scripture. She hopes to glorify God with her stories and inspire the next generation to discover the transformative power of God's Word.

COLLECT THE WHOLE SERIES!
*To get updates on new releases,
sign up for my newsletter at www.arabellapenrose.com*

Thank You!

Dear reader,

I hope reading this rhyming bible story inspired you and your child as much as it did me in writing it.

If you found value in this book, please consider leaving an honest review on Amazon or Goodreads. Your feedback helps other families discover meaningful books. And, by sharing your thoughts, you encourage me to continue writing stories that nurture little hearts.

Thank you for reading this timeless tale of Esther with your child. I'm grateful for readers like you.

Blessings,

Arabella Penrose

HAVE A PRAYER REQUEST
or want to reach out?
Email me at arabella@arabellapenrose.com

www.ingramcontent.com/pod-product-compliance
Lightning Source LLC
Chambersburg PA
CBHW041405010526
44107CB00015B/1075